Waking Dreams
DONNA L. POTTS

salmonpoetry

Published in 2012 by
Salmon Poetry
Cliffs of Moher, County Clare, Ireland
Website: www.salmonpoetry.com
Email: info@salmonpoetry.com

Copyright © Donna L. Potts, 2012

ISBN 978-1-907056-93-2

All rights reserved. No part of this publication may be reproduced or transmitted in any form or by any means, electronic or mechanical, including photography, recording, or any information storage or retrieval system, without permission in writing from the publisher. The book is sold subject to the condition that it shall not, by way of trade or otherwise, be lent, resold or otherwise circulated without the publisher's prior consent in any form of binding or cover other than that in which it is published and without a similar condition, including this condition, being imposed on the subsequent purchaser.

COVER ARTWORK: *Charles Wright*
COVER DESIGN: *Siobhán Hutson*

for Cecilia and Isabella

Acknowledgements

Acknowledgments are due to the editors of the following in which some of these poems first appeared:

New Hibernia Review, seveneightfive, Exposed, Moondance, Kansas City Star Magazine, and Poetry Digest.

Contents

Cigar Box	11
Pansies	12
Waking Dreams	13
Words for Rain	15
Missouri Blues	17
Other People's Rooms	18
Tiananmen Square, 2002	19
Burren	20
Licorice Line	21
Kansas Fall	22
Monarchs Migrating	23
Zinnias	24
Artemisia	25
The Gardens of Fort Worth	26
Tulipomania: The Wind Trade	27
Knot Tying	29
Another Mother for Peace	31
Ars Poetica	32
In Praise of Dreams	33
Cliffs of Moher	35
Cecilia's Poem	36
Kitchen Sestina	37
Concón	39
Trying Times	40
Snow Drops	41
Lily of the Valley	42
Sonnet in April	43
Haircut	44
Spring Storm	45
Aubade on a Summer Sunday	46
Surprise Lilies	47
Queen Anne's Lace	48
Tin Man	49
Starts and Stops	50

Domestic Violence	51
Growing Up	52
Night Terror	53
Agoraphobia	54
Target Christmas	56
Bothar na Miasa	57
Chicory	58
Manna	59
Prescriptive Grammar	60
Singing Snowbird	61
Castle Rock	62
Dylanesque	63
Iceland	64
Help	66
About the author	69

Cigar Box

When my dad was a boy some old uncle
gave him a cigar box full of pocket knives,
and he buried it in the backyard.
Every time I go to my hometown and drive by
the place where the house used to be,
I think of the box full of knives
and wonder if I could still uncover any sharpness,
if I could find the right place to dig and could force through
the crazed earth to the clay below, could I recover the boy
with the impulse to bury everything he loved,
who cocooned himself under the table
and fell asleep when fights broke between his parents
about letters from women that came while his dad was at war?

Pansies

I dream I'm surrounded by family
who suddenly vanish except for
my great uncle Virgil, long dead.
He takes me for a ride in the semi
he'd driven in life, except we go skyward,
along a track through a narrow tunnel,
with creaking fits and starts
like a Zurich funicular.
We step into a Technicolor Teletubby land,
with hills as green and gradual as Ireland,
no walls to mark out houses and rooms—
only carpets of flowers—pansies colored
lemon and grape and tangerine.
As soon as I say *it must never freeze here*,
I wake from what must have been my death dream,
my died-and-gone-to-heaven dream.
Pansy from *pensée*, French for thought—
a penny for your thoughts, for your pansies—
and I think of Virgil, my guide,
who aged into forgetfulness of everything
save the woman he'd loved and lost.
He coaxed squirrels into his house
with sunflower seeds, and left them to climb curtains
while he wandered streets looking for her,
who lived on only in his mind.
In my next dream I form pansies
into a bouquet for a love now lost.
Their feathered edges flutter
in the freezing wind
as I hand them over.

Waking Dreams
for Richard

"Is my life a dream?" he asks,
"Because sometimes I think I imagined
this world and I'll wake up in the real one."
He asks as though I'm big enough
to be entrusted with such vast questions,
as though I'd been hiding the truth all along,
waiting only for him to guess it.
How could I answer him, then or ever?

With intellect, perhaps, which cooks
every rawness to some safe temperature?
I could say, yes, son, philosophers have
pondered this one for centuries,
and trot out big guns like Plato and Plotinus,
or flowery lines about waking dreams,
how we're such stuff as dreams are made on,
how our life is but a sleep and a forgetting,
and our path emerges from a misty dream.

Or I could answer with my heart,
that there's a dark night of the soul
from which we fear we'll never awaken.
And I hear my mother's chanting cries when
my father's body was found hanging from a bridge,
"this is all a bad dream, all a bad dream,
and someday I'll wake up." I see
my years of trying to wake myself up,
running for any pain I could find,
dying to be in over my head.

Or I could answer with my soul, and say,
"sometimes I think I dreamed you up,
with your fair hair, your tenderness and wit,

so unlike your parents, yet so like
the grandfather you will never meet.
I dreamed you just to quell a longing in myself
to steal back time and fix what had gone wrong,
just my way of playing the hero,
the time traveler who arrives on the scene
just before the world explodes."

But he's too young for any of this,
as are we all, and whether dream or real,
it's his life to live, not mine, so instead I say,
some people like to think we live in dreams,
so they can hope to wake to something better,
leaving him to imagine his own heaven,
hoping it's within me to spare him some hell.

Words for Rain

One April morning,
five minutes before he has to leave for class
if he's to make it on time,
which he seldom does,
my son announces,
"I need a poem. What should it be about?"
I look out the kitchen window,
where it's been raining
in sheets, in blankets, for days,
and say, "write about rain."
"Is this for English class?"
I ask hopefully, because that's what I teach,
but he says, "No, it's for French,"
a language I've never learned
beyond ordering in restaurants.
I know only that rain is one of those Germanic words
for which there are no cognates
in other branches of Indo-European,
and sure enough, the word for rain in French is *"la pluie,"*
giving us *flow* and *flood*,
growing godlike in *Pluto*,
reigning in the realm of the dead,
his overflowing riches ever growing.
It also gives us *float* and *fly* and *flee*,
those words for drifting silently,
on or as though on water.
But he needs other words for rain in French,
and the word for "shower" is *douche*,
which he says he won't be caught dead
using in a poem or anywhere else.
"What if you said the sky is crying,"
which is what the great Elmore James said it does,
and it's what I feel like doing now:
"the sky is crying, look at the tears roll down the street."

Begin with *Le ciel pleure*.
Soon he will fly from me, he will flee this place,
and one day both of us will enrich
the hoard of the god of the dead,
but for now we sit at the kitchen table
searching for words for rain.

Missouri Blues

He skulked around town in a fake leopard skin coat,
except on Latvian Independence Day, when he wore a suit
that dared anyone to ask, "What's the occasion?"
He talked with a stammer, except, she discovered,
in the bathtub, where they'd sit eating rye bread
and listening to blues. To take these baths with her,
he crawled through the bedroom window after dark
twice a week, though it would have been simpler, quieter
and far less conspicuous simply to use the front door,
homage to her unwitting rehearsal to leave
a mean-streaked man working nights
at the underground storage.

He said he'd never own more than would fit in two suitcases,
not even books, that you gotta be black to sing the blues,
that romantic love was a capitalist plot,
all the while singing his blues and saying he loved her.
He talked about Canada, where he grew up,
and Latvia, where he came from,
until his pet cat loyal as any dog, and his
bread-baking Latvian grandmother were
as real to her as the cats that prowled her childhood,
as her one-armed Great Uncle Virgil
seining for shad on the Grand Lake of the Cherokees.

Fifteen years later, a picture of her with her children
hangs in his room in north Ontario,
and he still sends the books he buys and reads,
but will not permit himself to keep, so whether
in rain-soaked Ireland or sun-scorched Kansas
she follows him through snowy Saskatchewan,
across the blunt grey rocks of St John's
where the sun flashes everything in gold,
thinking how time passes, and doesn't,
of what love is, and isn't.

Other People's Rooms

"Come to my room and I'll give you my book,"
the poet said, laying a hand on the back of her neck
"I won't do anything." She thought,
Nothing that hasn't been done before, recalling
unwelcome hands up gingham dresses on hot days,
a preacher's kisses neither asked for nor returned,
a professor's fingers forcing past a wall of grief
into a shell pink sea garden,
and then the pronouncement
that cut the tongue right out of her:
"I have a lot of power in this department,
so it won't do you any good to say anything."
She doesn't speak for years,
lives on other people's words,
until one day she sees it for herself—
power and the hands it's placed into,
as well as the mouths it shuts.
She has no need to go to
other people's rooms for poems.

Tiananmen Square, 2002

No talk of tanks.

We're told they fly kites here, practice tai chi,
take pictures backdropped with Forbidden City
and a hugely looming Chairman Mao.
Scammers swarm toward round-eyes like us.
Street-vending hoards, to which we're taught to say
bu yao—don't want—sell fake Rolexes,
watches with waving Maos,
plastic Chinese flags, ice cream for children.
Our guide explains, "People from the country.
Blond hair, blue eyes new to them,"
as hundreds of hands fly to our children,
one line snaking toward my son, another, longer,
toward my daughter,
who waves her plastic flag,
Mao smirking over her shoulder,
caught by Chinese cameras for later release
in photo album fields.
One father proudly
places beside her a small sullen son,
who looks into the unfamiliar blue, and screams.

Burren

Sheets of stone for miles
until I learn to look in crevices
for wild thyme, gentians, rock roses.
Lying down I inhale a crush of herbs,
swallow heat from sunned rocks,
touch hidden, silken petals.

Further on, a throng of ferns,
a dark pool I want to wade into,
knowing well I will never return
to dry land—
butterfly weed,
purple coneflowers,
bright, unambiguous zinnias.

Licorice Line

I dreamed I asked him if he liked licorice,
and if he answered "yes" he'd be my lover.
Yes I will yes, he said, and bought me some in Lindsborg,
settled by Swedes who liked it salty sweet.
His name meant "cold" in Irish,
but he was all habañero and smoke
and Solomon's song spices,
hair black as licorice whips in sunlight
on our slow drive back down dirt roads.

One either loves or hates licorice, and
every Easter my mother and I fought
over black jelly beans others passed up
for brighter but blander bubble gum pink,
cherry red, lemon yellow, garish grape—
red "licorice"* whips good for nothing
but whiskers on some Betty Crocker Easter bunny cake.
She told me you could tell how
a man made love by how he ate.

There's a "licorice line" across Europe drawn by love
of licorice, dividing North and South, splitting
the language tree between Germanic and Romance.
I dream of solemn northerners swathed in wool
savoring licorice roots, chewing salty *drop***
shaped like fish or farm animals
until the descent of their last end of sweetness,
their southern cousins in sheer pastels,
light vowels rising like spun sugar
as they feast on marshmallows,
marzipan, meringues—
frothy confections
that leave me, teeth on edge,
hungry for a licorice lover.

---

* Red licorice is not really licorice.
** *Drop* is the name for the salty licorice that Northern Europeans prefer.

Kansas Fall

*"I live in another world where life and death
are memorized.
Where the earth is strung with lovers' pearls and all
I see are dark eyes."*
      BOB DYLAN

I memorize him like a poem I love,
a few lines at a time—
smile lines around dark eyes,
hands that learn me line by line,
the line of a foot pushed purposefully
against a windowsill as he names
himself for me in a soft drawl
that makes me love the state I'm in.

I memorize him as a charm
to carry in old age,
remembering my great grandmother
at 100, too deaf and blind for
talk and television to reach,
saying over and over
the poems she learned as a girl.
Soft heart locked in a bone box
with only poems and memories for company,
and a mouth the only unfailing means
for recalling the smell of sex,
the sound of ecstasy, the feel of warm skin,
the sight of a small bed in a corner
outside of which, for a time,
nothing of any consequence existed.

Monarchs Migrating*

Sunday in October. I've decided to leave my husband.
My mother, knowing nothing of my plan,
has decided to take us to a Renaissance festival in her car.
Like a dutiful daughter, I've told her I'm happily married,
assured her he only insults me when he's around her.
He sits in the back, I, in the front, where I have far too good a view
of the monarch migration. They struggle south, reaching for warmth,
while we drive directly into their flight,
haplessly crushing hundreds of fragile bodies
against our windshield. Before there is time
to see design in black and orange,
their papery forms have dissolved against glass.
I want to scream to stop the car,
sure if I don't do something,
some inner force will fling me toward them.
He's threatened to kill me if I ever left him,
said no one else would want me,
found my body good for spending only,
my words no more than stops and starts of breath
against the hard wall of the world.
From where I sit, rebirth and death seem the same.
Weighing my options, I fly.

---

* Many American monarch butterflies migrate in the fall, wintering in the mountains in Mexico.

Zinnias
for Lydia

Before I left for college we planted zinnias
that burst in profusions of saffron and cherry,
peach and plum, sat before them for a picture,
arms locked against all takers.

I filled my new room with any brightness
I could find, the shot of us in summery stripes,
the orange laundry basket,
your going away gift
that cost your eight-year life savings.
In winter, where once was home,
our garden gone to seed,
father taken by his own hand,
mother out of range, and you —
you fell as you ran to me,
scraped your knee, cried for life.

Back in my dark room,
I wait for something to develop,
see only a basket for washing,
a photo of sunny faces
safe from winter in a garden
all mind, no matter now.

Artemisia
for my mother

Wormwood is its other name.
Chalk-white in sunlight, toothy leaves
turning to slick pine when wet,
Artemisia smells like licorice, like
Asian lilies—sharp and spicy-sweet.

Yet within its lacy silver sway
this healing herb hides heavy truth.
The God of Jeremiah once decreed
the diet of the disobedient
would be wormwood and gall.

Poets in Paris cafes, slumped
over cups of its milky abstract,
Absinthe, found the bane beneath the beauty,
woke too soon from dim musings
to convulsive awareness.

Yet its stems are pliant,
its dried leaves delicate as fern.
See how patient fingers, death defying,
shape them into scented silver wreaths,
softening sharp angles, daunting the moth.

The Gardens of Fort Worth*

The Fort Worth Municipal Rose Gardens began in 1933,
with cash and roses donated by Fort Worth elite,
and labor provided by the WPA.
A local professor lectured on
"Fall Rose Planting and New Flowering Shrubs"
for the well-heeled citizens of Riverside.
The former Barbara Hutton,
granddaughter of the 5 and 10
Fort Worth Woolworth,
became Princess Mdivani
when she married a prince
of Georgia under the Russians.
At his 5th avenue home
there was a Hungarian orchestra,
a program of opera singers,
supper at small tables for
fifty guests of Barbara's age.
That November a visitor to Fort Worth
observed six-year-old boys selling
papers and magazines on the street,
"in their bare feet and with no other clothing
but overalls and little cotton waists,"
and, at 17, my great aunt began selling
herself to men who placed orders
from the Blackstone Hotel.

* The Fort Worth Botanical Gardens originated with the rose gardens, planted in 1933. (from the Fort-Worth Star Telegram, November, 1933)

Tulipomania: The Wind Trade

In the Ottoman Empire, tulips grew wild,
springing, the story goes, from the blood
of a prince falsely told his lover had been killed,
symbols of perfect, perfectly deluded love.
Tulips were worn in turbans,
painted on water bottles,
stitched on prayer rugs, soldiers' underclothes,
to stave off misfortune.
When Christians fought Muslims
on the plain of Kosovo, severed heads
in bright turbans filled the field,
looking to some like a giant tulip bed.

Holland's first bulbs came from Istanbul,
a gift to a merchant, who looked at the brown
anonymous packages, and decided to eat them
like onions, roasted and seasoned with oil and vinegar,
planted the rest in his kitchen garden,
where they sprang up red and yellow in spring,
until which no Dutchman had ever seen a tulip,
after which they all grew wild for them.
Single bulbs served as bride's dowries,
bought taverns and shops;
Bulbs still in the ground bought and sold
so often their sale was called "the wind trade"—
a price made of thin air.
The rarest tulips, called "Rembrandts"
for gracing his paintings, were the most beautiful,
with marbled flower heads of red shot with silver,
purple velvet streaked with yellow satin,
their beauty's secret source a virus.
One day in Haarlem, the greater fool refused to pay,
and the mirage of tulip mania faded.

Centuries later, Kansas suddenly sodden
with rain, from my rock garden planted with
red tulips, my husband's first Valentine gift,
a Rembrandt tulip sprang—
crimson stripes on neon yellow,
its ragged turban balanced
precariously on a thin stem.

Knot Tying

> "The clove hitch can be termed as indispensable. It is the one you have to be able to do with closed eyes, in the middle of the night, with your hands behind your back or in a plaster cast, and in water above your head."
>
> THE ART OF KNOT TYING

At the craft store down the street,
women tie knots to form patterns to
decorate pillowcases and pictures.
But when the Fates ruled uncontested,
knot tying was an art, an enchantment
beyond all learning. Knots that double as chairs,
Cinquefoils, French shrouds, Turk's Heads—
All amaze—but can't compare with windknots
tied with enchantment by Lapland witches
to bring fair winds with their untying,
or Ulysses' knot, closed with Circean art
to secure rich robes, vases, gold.

Fishing in Oklahoma with my father
just past a rainbow sign announcing
"Grand Lake of the Cherokees,"
I tied fisherman's knots in nylon line
to hold icy buckets of shad,
stringers of catfish and crappie.
Along the shore were fish scales
like translucent shells my teacher
brought from places I had never been.
Bait boxes of wood and window screen
housed elegant grasshoppers in tails,
blowing black tobacco bubbles.
The grit of a boat dragged through rocks,
bird calls like questions never answered,
still echo beyond the last knot he tied—
the hangman's—near the place we once fished.

These days, knots prove unreliable—
Ties bind all too tightly—
Slip knots loosen when they shouldn't,
tighten beyond my strength for untying,
leaving me no choice but to cut through.
On television, actors reenact crimes—
Women bound and gagged are later untied,
predictably, by placid policeman-actors who
then bind unbending criminal-actors—
which all fits into an hour-time slot
comfortably.

I tie and untie my own knots, endlessly,
pretending I can confound the fates, whose
withered fingers still hold the thread.

Another Mother for Peace
(i.m. C.R.)

She stood in the Kansas cold holding
her daughter's hand, holding a sign
they'd made together that read,
"another mother for peace."
Opposite them were students in
lawnchairs holding signs that read,
"Nuke Iraq" and "Bomb Iraqis."
Found dead in a house pooling with blood,
victim of the county's most brutal murder,
she'd dared to love someone other than her husband,
who called himself the "original boy scout,"
told detectives the bumps and scratches on his hands
had come from "roughhousing with his daughter,"
who told detectives she didn't like to roughhouse.
She liked to play with dolls, and have tea parties.
He'd searched the internet to learn
how to kill someone quickly and quietly,
how to murder without getting caught.
Rage grew, war broke, and the voice
of just another mother for peace was silenced,
just another child left motherless, fatherless.

Ars Poetica

"All you have to do to write a poem is look out a window"

You may have to look out a window to write a poem,
but that's only the first step.
First you must find the right window,
and then continue to look for years,
ever mindful of all who've looked out before you,
yet still give the impression that you're
the first who's ever truly seen what lies beyond.

And of course you must look at something,
then say what that something is, even when
it's dark and foggy, even when you cannot see to see.
And you must find a way of showing all the others
who aren't at the window exactly what there is to see,
and convincing those who really don't care to see
that they're missing the sight of a lifetime.

You might even wish to show it so plainly
that even their children and children's children
can feel that they, too, have looked out that very window,
even long after the window is gone.
And sometimes you might have to toss your heart
right out that window, like a child's ball,
just to get people to look up in wonder,
only to watch someone kick it aside,
without even glancing up to see its owner.

In Praise of Dreams
after Wistawa Szvmborska

In my dream
Philip Larkin comes to life in a wax museum,
pronouncing me among the less deceived.

I speak fluent Greek
with shepherd-poets
on green Sicilian hillsides.

I drive a car
with Seamus Heaney
to a country of the mind.

I am gifted
as Roethke or Bishop at soothing
a painful past into sestinas, villanelles.

I hear voices
of long dead poets
and they hear mine.

My piano performances
respond to the syncopations
of Hughes' jazzed up dream poems.

I fly the way prescribed,
like the soul in "The Seafarer,"
over the ocean's paths.

Falling off a roof
I swoop safely to shelter
landing on leaves of grass.

Breathing under water
I swim like a stippled fish to shore
on Innisfree's purple-heathered Isle.

I'm not complaining:
I know the Beautiful Changes
as the forest is changed.

It's a pleasure always,
however, to distill divinest sense,
to write the poem that changes the world.

Immediately war starts,
but when my poem is read above the thunder
peace appears like sudden sunlight through scant clouds.

I exist, but don't have to be
fastened to a dying animal
my hungry heart howling, biting at air.

Some years ago
I was gathered into the artifice of eternity,
somewhere well out, beyond, and saw the Happy Isles.

And the day before yesterday a penguin,
Neruda's magellanic priest of the cold,
stood beside Stevens' snowman, glittering in the sun.

Cliffs of Moher

Black Cliffs,
white waves,
gales that throw us
toward them.
You grab my hand
and pull me from the path,
where we huddle until the wind dies.
I remember Iowa when I was your age,
wind so strong
across the fields
I thought I'd blow away,
then dreamed I had.
Wind picks my up
And carries me
until I learn to turn
abduction into flight:
My strong sure wings
take me over farmhouses
scattered like white chicklets,
gold and green chessboard fields,
toy cars grown too tiny to give fright.
I land safely in bed,
wake to remember
a world where winds
blow at my bidding.

Cecilia's Poem

"Time to get up! I turned the sun on,"
you cry at dawn, marching in to our room,
switching on lights, waking us.
You say birds sing because they think
your dress is pretty, and draw pictures
with suns that smile on people clothed in rainbow,
chimneys with smoke rising in deft silver curls
from houses in which someone's always home
and always glad to see you.
When your big brother asks
if your friend's new house is cool,
you say, "yes, you can turn on the fire with a switch.
The wood isn't real, but the fire is.
Her house is on Puddle Creek
and has two kittens in it."
Selecting a name for your soccer team,
you choose "Golden Butterflies," deaf to
your brother's jeers, because your jerseys are
a mustard yellow you prefer to see as golden.

At night, with lights out,
your eyes stay open as long as they can,
not for fear or uncertainty, but for
not wanting to miss anything in this world,
brighter for your vision.

Kitchen Sestina

I spent all day in the kitchen making a meal,
a teenage dish of chicken tetrazzini
for my family, who'd just spent their day
slaughtering chickens raised on our land.
No wonder they had no appetite for dinner,
having just wrung the necks of kin.

Cooking with kin has never been easy.
At family fish fries my great aunt's
hard scrabble truth landed on us
just before dinner: "if any of you young-uns choke
on a bone, don't count on *us* to stop the meal to save you,"
a bitter dish for small mouths to swallow.

As a child I ate dishes of cornflakes with chopsticks,
practicing for faraway lands I hoped to visit,
feeding my kin from the UNICEF cookbook,
forcing meals of borsht, injera, guava toast
on my baffled midwestern family,
soon too afraid to ask "what's for dinner?"

When I made a last-minute dinner for a date—
a family favorite—tuna and noodle casserole,
with frozen broccoli thrown into the dish
to make him think I valued nutritious meals,
he ate four helpings, and I felt a kindred
spirit had landed for life.

Life in other lands, different kitchens,
brought new dishes—
meals of curry bunnies in South Africa,
Chinese dinners of fish, eyeballs and all.
Kinship kept us through sushi and kimchee,
with chocolate the family tie that bound.

At 13, my son became the family cook,
had dinner ready when I got home late,
dishes of fish and chips, potato soup,
Ireland's bounty put to good use.
His younger sister, next of kin, made her
first meal too, cheddar soup and soda bread.

Meals dished out
for dinner; kindnesses
that make any land familiar.

Concón

"Si como caminas cocinas, guardame el concón." *

Working for a newspaper in the Dominican Republic,
he learned they had a word that could refer
either to the crisp rice clinging to the bottom of the pot,
regarded as delectable, or to an enticing woman.

"Concón," he said, dark amber eyes shining
as they had in class all those years ago,
and she knew but for the ring on her finger,
he'd use that word on her.

Today she makes rice for her children,
her husband, leaving it on the flame
a little too long, scooping out
the soft white rice for them,
scraping out the darkened, crisp remains
for herself, remembering jasmine,
summer breeze, swimming pools,
amber eyes closed for good now,
letting the concón linger on her tongue.

---

* A popular pick-up line in the Dominican Republic, which translates as, "If you're going to the kitchen, save the concón for me."

Trying Times, 2005

There has been no Revolution.
Dubya peers out from the *Irish Times*
looking for all the world like the village idiot.
In my "home" state of Kansas, Fred Phelps
the Preacher proclaims (on his "God Hates
Fags" website) the Tsunami to be the fault
of evil people everywhere
and concerned citizens hold their monkey trial
while California tries its moonwalking pedophile,
and Florida fights to save one brain-dead white
woman, while three white police officers
handcuff a five-year-old black girl who
won't do her math. "Family values" folks
condemn Spongebob for his gay lifestyle,
after horrified witnesses testify they saw him
holding hands with a pink starfish named Patrick.
With wars and rumors of war on all fronts,
there still has been no Revolution.
People are too busy picking fights.

Snow Drops

Our earliest flowers
bloom clean as the snow
that sometimes obscures them,
softening harsh lines of
ice-sheathed branches, brittle grass.
Silent bells tolling in the season,
starters for spring's fine feast.

Lily of the Valley

> *"leaf-sheltering lilies of the valley…will keep in tiny, exquisite bells their secret clapper."*
> MONA VAN DUYN

In belfries of gray green,
perennially proliferating,
hang fragile white bells,
silent but for scent
insistent and pure
enough for perfume,
annointing oil.
bridal bouquets,
fading by June.

Sonnet in April

(In memory of Ronald F. Potts, 1939-1981)

After the snowdrops, during the daffodils,
we'd fish for croppie—my father and I.
He'd carry me across the shallows
to a bank where we'd stay up all night,
a Coleman lantern our only light.
I drank my first coffee then: cold Folgers
from an old thermos. As I grew up and away
I'd fish for other things in books I brought.
After the snowdrops, during the daffodils,
thirty golden Aprils spent, I see the bank
by lantern light, silver fish in a seine,
small rocks waiting to be skipped,
cane poles bowed hopefully, ever out of reach,
now there's no one to carry me across.

Haircut

"You don't even know how lovely you are,"
a man told her when she was twenty-one,
and she shrugged and walked away,
sure that with so many dead lying round
she was damaged goods best left unopened.
All the lovely things were wrapped gifts with
someone else's name on the tag,
locked boxes lined up waiting for
someone else to arrive with a key.

She didn't know how the heart,
when healing, reveals hidden chambers,
how the soul, when struck,
rings out its surprising range.
The darkest chambers of Newgrange
make way for light, reveal design
most strikingly on the shortest day,
just when light seems gone for good.

Years later, in line at a coffee shop
a young man in front has just had a haircut,
turns around when someone at the counter
wants a look at the back.
He's coming out of hiding,
out from under a dark cloud,
scribbling poems that say between lines,
damaged goods, not the brightest crayon in the box.

It's June and all she sees is light,
in yellow hair, blue eyes
that meet hers and linger there –
primary colors she chose in childhood,
jeweled fruit her uncle hauled from Texas.
And she longs to say,
you don't even know how lovely you are,
you don't even know.

Spring Storm

As the clouds grew heavier,
she remembered the way
the air goes quiet and electric
just before a storm,
the way people stand on the edge
of something happening.
Then she found her way to him.
Now she'll remember the way
cold rain blew in on them
from the open window,
the way lightning lit his body,
the way rain hid her tears.

Aubade on a Summer Sunday

The sun rises too early these days.
Birds begin their insistent songs,
but we sleep through sun and songs
until the blare of the clock radio
bleeds into the bedroom,
a preacher of the gospel
who predicts hell fire,
global catastrophe,
for the likes of us.
We were up until near dawn
listening to a *Love Supreme*,
watching *The Rules of the Game*
breaking the rules in what
was no longer any game.
I could linger to praise each part,
your shocked black hair and dark eyes,
the linen luster of your skin,
the smooth spot on the back of your neck
that smells like cinnamon and rum
that I usually have to tiptoe to kiss,
now as near me as my next breath.
The meadow of your backside,
unsheeted by the heat,
could hold me for years
but I have to leave for a life
that's no longer mine,
for demands I can't meet,
while uneasy gospel music plays—
calling, "oh sinner, come home."

Surprise Lilies
(i.m. Howard Nemerov)

Springtime brings the foliage
strong and green as any other lily's,
but fading flowerless.
In autumn, just when it seems
no lilies are left in this world,
sturdy stems break through
hard cracked summer soil
bearing sunset colored flowers
lasting as any other lilies,
though dearer because more hoped for,
more rare amid the fall foliage
of umber and amber, embering out.

Queen Anne's Lace

So much depends
upon

a green glass
vase

filled with Queen Anne's
Lace

gathered from Ohio
fields

on the highway home
to Kansas.

Tin Man

Because he was not putty in her hands,
an open book, a breeze, a cinch, much less
a piece of cake, she decided he was asphalt—
dense and dark—a hard surface—
but one that absorbed heat, softened slowly.
When she found that nothing warmed him nor soaked in,
she decided he was a mirror—
a hard surface—
but one that reflected the watchful
on its shimmering silver face.
But the glass was gray and tarnished,
and, moving closer, she found not
glass at all, but corrugated tin—
a hard surface, heavy, sharp-edged,
deflecting everything, revealing nothing.
Nor could it be reached into or around
without pain.
If kept at a safe distance,
could it be a roof against the rain?
or simply something best left lying
rusting and unused
in a recess outside her house?

Starts and Stops

It all started in the car, when he reached over,
touched her face and whispered,
"I've had such a crush on you."
Or maybe it started three years before,
when she noticed him in a coffee shop.
Wan faced, shock haired, he'd returned
her shy "hello" with stunned silence,
but never stopped studying her reflection.
When he left one day in his thin jacket,
purchased for California, not Kansas,
his back stiffening against cold,
she wanted to buy him a coat,
and maybe it started when she bought the coat,
and gave it, with a note, "please see he has a coat
so warm to keep him from the howling wind,"
and he cried and said "I love you,"
and wore the coat all winter,
even when it wasn't especially cold.
Or maybe it started when they sat on the couch,
legs wrapped together, and he nudged
her neck with his head like a little goat,
without needing words for what he wanted.
Or in the bathtub by candlelight
when they slid silkenly into each other,
warming as the water cooled and drained,
Or when they started trying to put into words
why and when and how they should stop it,
only to find that this time she was the
one without any words.

Domestic Violence

The soccer mom in sunglasses,
tall and tanned and lean,
arrives late to her son's match,
pulling the latest model twin stroller
from the shiny mini-van.

Her husband sits across the field,
handsome, and a little too loud.
From match to match the distance
will grow louder.

From his seat in the bleachers,
he shouts at his son, who flinches,
frail in his nylon uniform,
running as fast as he can,
but never fast enough.

The soccer mom could tell you,
if you asked, the Prada sunglasses
conceal bruises, all that her husband
would eventually leave her.

Growing Up

The picture's full of plush green grass glimmering
with pink and orange flowers over which
a jeweled rainbow's end draws the eye down
to a silver winged fairy in the corner.

Walk closer, if you dare, and see the flowers
become eyes that scrutinize, the fairy only
a model cut from some magazine, whose
airbrushed sleek perfection's only glamor.

The picture's called "Growing Up,"
and as you walk toward it you
remember your own growing up:
one minute emparadised, innocent only insofar
as you're beneath the line of anybody's vision;
the next minute, all eyes upon you,
your body no longer your own,
the world's beauty blinks with
the eyes that take you in.

The less of you the better,
in this grown up world you're in.

Night Terror

A fear too big for dreams finds me.
I wake to my own screams, running
nowhere from a thing that slithers
even from memory's momentary hold.
Though I've flung it coffee cups in sleep,
it vanishes when I wake.
The man beside me finds some clues,
wakes to hear me beg it to
leave, leave me alone.
Slowly I recompose:

A thickset Rumpelstiltskin
crouches by my bed,
head down, face shadow-shrouded,
exacting my soul's labor
of dross turned gold
to throw in some foul hole
littered with broken dolls,
bones, dreams of home.

Awaiting his next visit,
I long to aim at back or neck,
or better yet, make him look at me
while, with steady gaze,
I force him through the floor,
the foundation, the ground—
all because I finally guessed his name.

Agoraphobia

Once he grew out of them,
she painted the tips of her son's cowboy boots
hot pink so his little sister could wear them
as though they were all her own.

She sewed her dresses—blue to match her eyes,
green to match the grass and trees she loved,
aqua speckled with pastel fish to remind her
of the sea they swam in once.

She promises she'll make her a quilt
from all the scraps, as her mother once made her,
so after she grows out of the dresses
she'll have bright reminders of them.

Out on the soccer fields, watching her boy play,
she hears the whispers of the soccer moms,
reminding her that nothing she does is ever right.
In this climate of extremes of hot and cold,
the girl will always be too warmly dressed,
not warmly dressed enough. The mother will be
damned if she does, if she doesn't, if she does.

She retreats inside cool white walls,
pulls down shades, and reads the girl a story,
where no eyes can penetrate,
no one can snipe that her book choices
are age inappropriate, too old-fashioned,
too gender-specific, too risque.
In this climate-controlled room,
the girl's clothes are always just right,
the mother's love safe from deconstruction,
that is, until the girl grows up and away
and the whispers begin again.

By then the quilt will be finished,
packed in the trunk she once carried off to college.
May her daughter take it out, wrap it around her
and know she had been, is, would always be, loved.

Target Christmas

Ahead
of her in line
a young man buys
Christmas in a box,
a disassembled metal tree
and shiny red ornaments
so perfect she can see herself.

His whole holiday
emerges before her
new and untainted,
the tree snaking upward,
ornaments floating into place
like a Mary Poppins miracle.

All her ornaments are old—
dented brass angels salvaged
from a bruised up first marriage,
tarnished silver bells handed down
during her second by a mother-in-law
who carefully labelled and dated
her children's handiwork,
now hanging beside her own—
the patchwork bell from sewing class,
ceramic angels painted in her giddy teens,
the paper angel her sister made to top the tree
when she lived with them in college
the year their son was born,
and finally, her own children's tattered paper
candy canes, snowflakes, wreaths and stars
adorned with their photos, smudged with their fingerprints.

As the young man loads
Christmas into his cold car
she pities him, until she recalls
the rood, the tree that speaks,
that takes on life of its own
only to offer it up for others.

Bothar na Miasa*
(for Moya Cannon)

As we pick our way across limestone plates
to reach St. Colman's well
she tells how his servant,
weak with hunger near the end of Lent,
complained to Colman
(apparently too holy to hunger),
who told him to pray hard for food.
King Guaire at his castle in Kinvara soon saw
his Easter feast rise up and fly
out the window:
plates and goblets and silver
laden with such succulence
sailed across the burren, landing safely
at the feet of the astonished servant.
The king and his men thundered after the feast
across the rocks to Colman's well,
where the imprints of the horses' hooves can still be seen.
But in the presence of St. Colman
the feast no longer mattered.

She reaches into her backpack and takes out
sandwiches and gingercake and tea with milk,
spreading the feast on a rock at the well.
We notice hoof prints on the rocks around us,
which she explains are fossils from a time
when the stones were beneath the waves.

Back in Kansas, as heat sears and soil cracks,
I open her book of poems;
Water from the holy well flows free.
Miles away, I can taste the feast.

* The Road of the Dishes

Chicory

(i.m. Joe Lambert 1938-2009)

One night when death kept her awake
she called him and he made coffee with chicory
the way they drank it down South
in Mississippi where he got his manners and his drawl.

Before he was a professor he was a preacher
until one Sunday when white ushers
removed three black guests,
and he'd stood up and said,
"if your heaven is segregated,
I'd just as soon not go there."
He told this story in class one day,
just as the moral majority revealed
itself to be neither, just as she was
trying to decide what, if any,
heaven she wanted.

Years later in Oklahoma she sees
fragile blue flowers by a roadside
scattered with Indian graves.
"Chicory," her mother tells her,
a Cherokee tonic for nerves.

Blue flower—symbol of impossible strivings,
from the Glass Menagerie's blue roses
to the blue flame of her father's eyes
before he self-destructed.
But the professor's eyes were also blue,
so blue his wife fell into them and stayed,
Blue sailors*—destined for some port beyond us all,
for some heaven where we might live in peace.

---

* Chicory flowers are also called "blue sailors."

Manna

for Isabella and Laura

Manna fell like a welcome snow.
Gathered and ground and baked
into honeyed wafers, it kept the Israelites
through forty years of wilderness,
but wouldn't keep through the night,
festering with worms and death reek.

In the seaside town of Santa Margherita Ligure
we walk past lawns luxuriant with basil and rosemary
until we find focaccia, inhale its herbed heat.
An old woman warns us it will lose its savour
if taken from the salt sea air.

In Savannah we buy beignets
light as air and angels.
The woman behind the counter
cautions us to eat them right away;
before they turn back to dough,
as a coach once turned to pumpkin.

My small daughter reaches for me,
flinging tiny arms around me,
whispering "I love you."
As I lift her, light and sweet,
I take the moment while I have it,
knowing well what won't keep.

Prescriptive Grammar

Use "set" for transitives and "sit" for intransitives:
After setting fire to the house,
sit in the woods and watch it burn.

Use "lay" for transitives and "lie" for intransitives:
Leaving her lying in a pool of blood,
lay the knife down on the table.

Use "hung" for things and "hanged" for people:
As my mother hung the laundry,
my father hanged himself from a bridge.

Shall we save "shall" and "will" for another day?
Will it suit you?

Singing Snowbird

That summer Snowbird plays non-stop
on all the country stations
from Missouri to Oklahoma as we
drive to Grand Lake, my grandfather
at the wheel. He's been drunk so often
we don't know how sober sounds
as he slurs along with his favorite song -
spread your wings and fly away
and take the snow back with you
where it came from on that day.
He swerves down roads that snake
past bait shops, grocery stores, Indian graveyards.
My small sister sits in back, seeing
only the sweets from the shop we'd stop at soon,
but I can see him always in the driver's seat
while we sit helpless, sense his special disdain
for girls who'd begun to think for themselves.
Years later I'll learn how after his wife died
he left his three children alone for weeks
while he went off with women,
then started having his own daughter
when he saw in her changing face she wasn't really his,
leaving my father afraid to father,
to drink anything stronger than coffee,
to make his death wish known.
One day, walking down the street,
father and grandfather long dead,
I'll hear Snowbird in my head,
the one I love forever is untrue,
and if I could, you know that
I would fly away with you.
By then I'll know what its like
to wish the snow gone,
to want to fly away, to lack wings.

Castle Rock

In summer we dove
from Castle Rock
into the creek below,
waded its shallows,
warmed on its banks.
Along a path nearby
we dug sassafras roots for tea,
gathered black walnuts.
One fall, on a giddy teenage walk
with my best friend, we saw
two lovers under a tree, in the act.
We turned and ran, landing
laughing in a pile of leaves,
somewhere underneath which,
we knew were mine shafts,
who knew how deep,
maybe endless.

Dylanesque

He walks into her office
armed with a cd player,
which he slams down on her desk,
flinging himself on the chair beside her.
With a flip of his ponytail,
he punches the start button to release
a pent-up young Dylan
pleading, "I want you."
He leans in to her and asks,
"Have you heard this before?"
She's not only heard it; she's lived it,
she wants to say.
She's a big girl all the way,
and she takes just like a woman,
with the crazy patterns on her sheets
all tangled up in blue and
the ghost of electricity howling
in the bones of her face at all hours,
keeping her awake,
and who among them ever
really wanted just to kiss her?
When she asks Little Boy Lost
to please crawl out her window.
she knows she sounds like all the
washed out horns in the world,
but she recalls too well how she breaks.

Iceland *

Go to Iceland with me—Reykjavik.
He kept saying it as though he knew
what he was talking about. Any time
he wasn't busy bailing out homeless people
jailed for petty crimes or dreaming how
to make abandoned houses habitable
he was running after me down Ninth street
like some rangy Mick Jagger in glasses,
some half-baked Orpheus hell bent on pulling me out.

Go to Iceland with me—Reykjavik.
Enthralled as I was by the Canadian
twist he gave his vowels, the way he lingered
longingly over the consonants, all I could see
when he said Iceland was a land of ice—
darkness and blinding blizzards thrown in for free—
Nothing for us but Old Icelandic Eddas
better read right here in a warm bed with a fire.

Go to Iceland with me—Reykjavik.
The full force of his refrain hits me
when I read that Iceland often ranks
as the world's happiest country.
Icelanders all aspire to be poets,
joking that one day they'll erect a statue
in the center of Reykjavik
to honor the one Icelander who never
wrote a poem. They're still waiting for
that person to be born. "Better to go barefoot
than without a book," they say, and in their
kind of cold, they're saying a mouthful.

Rather than fear darkness, Icelanders
embrace it, their imaginations firing from
the elves and dwarves that emerge from stones;
friends who thought they heard sounds of laughter
and clinking glasses found only waves
crashing against the cliffs and birds chirping.
Icelanders love failure just as much as darkness,
as long as one fails with the best of intentions.

An American gone native says he loves the way
hot water spouts from the ground like geothermal gold,
the way people invite him over for coffee
for no particular reason and talk for hours
about nothing in particular, the way on
a brisk winter day the snow crunches
under his feet like heaving styrofoam,
the way Icelanders applaud when the plane
lands just because they're happy to be home.
He loves the magical, otherworldly feeling of
swimming laps in the middle of a snowstorm,
but most of all he loves the darkness, which
he wraps around himself like a blanket.

* All that I know about Iceland is taken from *The Geography of Bliss*.

Help

She has "Helpless" stuck in her head.
That Neil Young song about a North Ontario town
reminds her of someone she once knew,
but can't help now, his face to the wall
of some ward, thin hands folded for good.

Someone no older than Neil Young
was when he wrote his song
sits in the grass near the library,
writing his own songs about willows weeping
and houses burning and two moons,
one for us and one for everyone else.

He cries in all the right places until
she can't think of him as an age.
Soon enough his songs burn
through dry leaves of grief,
locked chains on closed doors.
In spring the grass where he used to sit
is hopeful green stuff woven,
and oh, so many uttering tongues

DONNA L. POTTS was born and raised in the Ozarks—in Joplin, Missouri—and now lives in Manhattan, Kansas, where she teaches Old English, History of the English Language, Modern and Contemporary Poetry, and Irish Literature at Kansas State University. A Fulbright Lecturing award to the National University of Ireland in Galway (1997-98) provided her with more time to write, and she returned there on sabbatical in 2004-05. Although she has written extensively on the poetry of Howard Nemerov, Seamus Heaney, Moya Cannon, Nuala Ní Dhomhnaill, and others, *Waking Dreams* is her first book of poetry.